OPEN HAND FALLING

CRAIG SCOTT

MAD RUSH BOOKS

Open Hand Falling
Craig Scott

ISBN 978-1-300-99779-5
Published by Lulu.com

Cover design and layout by Laura Ostman Chernyavskiy
Cover photographs by David Tomaloff

Mad Rush Books
http://1of25.tumblr.com

What are you paranoid over now?

Blood, misuse, ennui.

I interpret candy bars & skin.

This is my life.

You are a mess
you
fucking
perfect
thing

I don’t do want some.
I do don’t want more.
I will won’t ask.
I won’t will take.
I can’t can go on.
I can can’t go on.

we see dragons = those w/halitosis are close talkers
I am flying in a blue balloon ~ I am falling in a rush of air
make a lunge - forget, not forget
see space / space sees more space
text no geez <= I know more technology that yr hair
yes =/ no

those those who those who sing those who those who
they they are rain & fire &

or naught null nill night nothing never
...

pan leftways & around the backside for yr panhandling gods
w/their magic toes & superstar lice

hijacking yr church's organ sheet music
selling the soles of 1 hundred feet

immature insolence
urbane odors

they don't know yr name
there's milt in yr green tea

it's Thor's day
it's a steel cage death match vs. yr brain's rationalizations

ration nation
rats ions zing

any1 who cares
can have it all

their promises & lies
their offspring & their dead

the godless move on
the gods move to the philippines

"I've never been to Scotland," she said.
"And you never will," I said.
"How can you be so cruel?" she said.

I went to the bathroom. "Why am I wearing yr underwear?" I said.
"You like them more than I do," she said.
"Yes," I said, "right."

give yr pus & stones to the wishing wells
yr quarters won’t work   here

make love to cardboard cutouts of Patrick Troughton
turgid embrace   b&w shenanigans

ride yr unicorn across yr ocean of confused inflection
we love you   know matter   what

happy

all aglow,
all alive,
all loved

xmas @ age 5 every other day
yr bday @ age 21 other every day

all you have to know is

nothing dies
until you do

a lighthouse
blinks

the fish don't mind the rain
the rain doesn't mind the fish

meanwhile
odd hair
runs an eight minute mile
across the sun

there are rumors of asteroids
& sensuous cossets

you can make up anything & they will believe it
you have one of those faces

sex games
sex gangs

no more weed for you

even so
membership waning

broken brown bear
seeking lonliness

you can run from cannibals
but not from the cameras in squirrels

red lips

forgive me

the soul
always+never

sex
temporary

a sword
bold

everyone is a chainsaw
except you

you are a goat
complex & falling into a pulsar

caramel & heels
together on my tongue
            I wish yr eyes on me
            I will yr body on mine

hands explode

alien invasion

I only go to whores who look like you

only when the world is in peril
so
always

we’re bi in hell
& hell is other people

enough sexual tension all the fish in the aquarium can swim in it

re   member
me
on yr   wedding night

forgive the sleeping dogs & their lies; lives; livers; lovers.

drink Kentucky women
& bourbon

∞.

a hole under the bed.

experiments, > dread?

I wrote this on my iPhone in the dark.

"We should all be so lucky."

Rush. More. Movie. Bodies.

ray   sun
river   bang
tall   tree
plastic   lip
couch   cough
pay   phone

let freedom go
&&
what smells here

: I miss you

move

make it happen

I can hear yr texts

harder

somewhere

inside

fill me

more

I ate 1 aardvark because my cysts were not in the mood to be social

I eat 10 jalapenos on a quest for hair loss

I ate 100 copper pieces to measure my humanity

I eat 1000 nipple rings because it's my birthday

I ate 10,000 blades of grass because glass & gum scare me

I eat 100,000 m&ms to learn yr blood type

I ate 1,000,000 websites to remember the actor who played Scaroth

I eat 1,000,000,000 curtains to save a landfill

I ate 1,000,000,000,000 $s because fuck you

&&&

& just
like   that

I was 20 lbs

            lighter

oral hope
text

new print(+) never

alpha ^fall

alive window ;laugh

power& fat facts

… *begin*

Fear my love me
you too holding
hands sucking off
toes too much
heat high humping
the zygote licking
the fur rhyming is
hard unnecessary
form begin end
conversion now

Fear|my|love|me
you|too|holding
hands|sucking|off
toes|too|much
heat|high|humping
the|zygote|licking
the|fur|rhyming|is
hard|unnecessary
form|begin|end
conversation|now

Fearmyloveme
youtooholding
handssuckingoff
toestoomuch
heathighhumping
thezygotelicking
thefurrhymingis
hardunnecessary
formbeginend
conversationnow

Public smile
        pubic intentions

I can taste the air sometimes
        when it's in trouble
I am ______ for you
        can you see ______
                would you want to ______

Pink hair rap lyrics you made it

Assess threat level - Brazilian culo cults - 69%
        2469

the world isn't perfect
& it doesn't have to be

Send:;:
        release!

I sense waffles drainage into the ocean
I feel obfuscated

I hear the swan gulping stale bread The man forming his tongue Paint waiting for
[[[[[[[XXXXXXX]]]]]]] to happen J in 8th grade science breathing
through her nose Gojira attacking Tom Servo in a poem I wrote in high school

idk what's next but I know how it ends

Don't mourn me when I'm gone
Sing me that I lived

This experiment to kill the sun

You wonder why
I go through with

open yrself to

Ebola
rot
opportunity

{ /// } is gone.

"Why are you not happy always?"
"Stop being observant."

Always a line
to
yr face

This is
incognito hair & a lisp

    Quoting a
    blind blonde in
    sweatpants

Order
Open

Execute the executioner

There is too much music in the world & not enough [   ]

Send requests to the crawlspace.

Open new.

Can I get a :?.

"This shirt is not flattering."

I wish you love & words.

Run, runner, to the end of time. On time.

This is. Just right

A door opens,
a jogger without pants.

"This is all
too
much"

says the snow.

Lemon yellow teeth, April showers,
a minivan driving in South Carolina.

Someone says something to a
calculator.

I love you but not in that
rape (*Brassica napus*).

Seduced & slandered
by

an inappropriate oral fixation
catfish barbels
heads like holes, black as souls
GMO foods
a hiccup
chiropractors
poems about me.

"In print it's libel."

Shut up.

This is ~~not~~ happening.

nude hungry
wet
open
more

:: rewind, ff, skip, rewind, ff, loop ::

& I'm done(twice).

I am just done
down
poking the red

ape nipples

milking mothers
hungry Venus fly traps

my X-ray goggles never came in the mail

"So this is you & us."

Begin.

"Hold, enough!"
(You lasted two line breaks. Yr score is now 3.4. Please p(l)ay again (not).)

We are both: Odin & the
document.

Plastic fever, soft to the touch. A doll in yr arms.

Wild hair
& women.

Wine her, dine her. Leave
alone.

Watch *Un Chien Andalou* for the seventeenth time this week
- seven teeth -

b/c you once poked a hand in the street & you don't
shave

yr eyes

(heads I win
tails you lose).

I don't care about mortgage rates or churches
or gluten-free cereal.

I am the last page in a book.
I am drying flowers nailed to the wall.
I am the fool who drinks raspberry seltzer on a Friday night.

I am jumping back & forth between Charon & Pluto.
I am disowned & having a grand ol' time.

Yes.
So,
goodnight.

Craig Scott is an unimaginative pseudonym. Craig is the real first name, Scott is the real middle name. Various projects have been done under this name, most recently the collaborative hardcover collection *Tales From a French Envelope* (w/ Catfish McDaris) and the chapbook *Garage on the Edge of Town* (Writing Knights Press). He edited the webzine *The*, the e-chap press Ten Pages Press, and the web/print zine *Mad Rush*. His latest project is the print zine *1/25* (http://1of25.tumblr.com). Poems and other work appear from time to time under this name as well, here and there, in print and online.

ALSO FROM MAD RUSH BOOKS

Magazines
1/25
Mad Rush

Collections
God's Will by Scott Urban
You Sang It Back to Me by Amanda Deo
Jupiter Orgasma by Catfish McDaris
Waiting on Nothing by Catfish McDaris
Punk Me by Patricia Hickerson
Tales From a French Envelope by Catfish McDaris & Craig Scott

http://1of25.tumblr.com
http://www.lulu.com/spotlight/madrush